Expressions Sanctioned by

GOD

Through the Eyes of
Amazing Grace

Expressions Sanctioned by
GOD
Through the Eyes of
Amazing Grace

GRACE S. THOMPSON

ARPress
ILLUMINATING IDEAS
EMPOWERING VOICES

ARPress
45 Dan Road Suite 5
Canton MA 02021

Hotline: 1(888) 821-0229
Fax: 1(508) 545-7580

Ordering Information:
Quantity sales. Special discounts are available on quantity purchases by corporations, associations, and others. For details, contact the publisher at the address above.

Printed in the United States of America.

| ISBN-13: | Softcover | 979-8-89356-660-4 |
| | eBook | 979-8-89356-661-1 |

Library of Congress Control Number: 2024903476

CONTENTS

CHAPTER 3: LIFE'S DEFINING MOMENTS AS THINGS CHANGE

CHAPTER 4: ESSENTIALS NECESSARY TO MOLD THE WHOLE PERSON

CHAPTER 5: TRIBUTES TO INSPIRATIONAL LEADERS

CHAPTER 6: SOUL SOOTHING WRITING IN THE PANDEMIC

Dedication

Dr Virginia Russell transitioned to her heavenly home this year after spending ten remarkable years with me living life to the fullest between the writing of book one and book two. The impact of her wisdom and teachings is printed in my heart. The face value of her as an advisor, Soror, friend and instructor lead me to dedicate this book in memory of Soror Russell.

God's presence is forever in my life and always will be. God keeps me anchored and guided by his plan.

I know no one else to trust or follow; therefore, I choose Jesus. He puts the right person in the right place at the right time. He allows special people's paths to cross. "He has a ram in the bush." I am so thankful for Belinda Evans, my ex-daughter -in law, who is smart, talented, and a scholarly partner. She is always ready and willing to make situations better. She speaks well and with authority, she enhances my writings, and says it the right way. So, as I think it, she says it perfectly.

Expressions Sanctioned by God through the Eyes of Amazing Grace is dedicated to Soror Belinda Evans and in memory of Ivy Beyond the Wall, Soror Virginia Russell for lots of sentimental reasons and a unique connection.

The Me I Desire To Be

I like to pattern myself after Jesus
I like to be humble and peaceful
Loving, kind, longsuffering and meek.
I want to have a smile for people I seek.

Exhibiting gentleness
Spreading. cheerfulness
Showing I am caring
Helpful and capable of sharing.

I feel my living isn't in vain
Mistreatment causes me great pain.
No part of me wants to be mean
Unity and harmony are my dreams.

If I keep the dream alive
I will be free from any jive.
It definitely would be perfected
For this is the path I'm directed.

Grace's Rainbow

My rainbow, filled with an array of colors
Each one represents a trait of me.

Yellow signifies my beautiful smile
That radiates happiness as far as the Nile.

Green symbolizes the inevitable or unknown
For once awareness evolves, I've grown.

Blue lets me know there is loneliness
After it passes, comes true happiness.

Violet denotes a mixture of colors or two
Helpfulness, kindness must shine through.

Orange carries the fire and the flame
Honesty and character both make a name.

Red signals there is some danger ahead
Precaution with amber or you'll be dead.

Beautiful rainbows seen on sunny days
Traits of a reputable woman need no pay.

Grace exhibits the colors of the rainbow
When the sun is high, a rainbow is low.

Near the horizon, you see the full circle
Just as the qualities in Grace Sparkles.

CHAPTER 1

FAMILY

God created man because he desires to have a family.
A group of people related to each other. A unit of people that support
and share each other's joys, sorrows, and successes.
A family is a place where principles are hammered
and honored on the anvil of everyday living.

Family

My family means the entire world to me
I will ever be so appreciative to thee.
For providing someone with whom to chat
You didn't send just any old bothersome brat.

A family member stands by in any situation
Much more than mere recreation
As trials come and all odds are against me
Family's encouragements bring me through.

Just take on some huge or challenging tasks
Watch it, your family hides behind no mask.
They spring up resourceful and in full bloom
My supportive family refuses to be doomed.

A family signifies love and togetherness
They will blot out most of your loneliness.
A family missing is neither joy nor real fun
Without it you'll act like some on the run.

My Daddy

My daddy was a good-hearted man
Lord, God Almighty was his favorite fan.
He used the bible to train his offspring
In the way they should go he did bring.

His huge garden's harvesting he shared
Teaching his seeds the same 'cause he cared
Accompanying them to church was his job
He allowed no one to separate him from God.

I thought daddy was mean many times
As I grew older I knew he saved us from crime.
He taught us how to work and care for ourselves
Daddy was firm, loving, kindhearted and rare

My daddy raised us as well as he did
Life's realities and mysteries were not hid.
I am a product of his divine teaching
Blessed to have been touched by his reaching.

A Mother

A mother is someone's miraculous wife
Responsible for giving to you the gift of life
Molding you with her special kind of brand.
Any actions you take put her in a twirl.

A mother always stand by your side
Even when you make the wrong stride.
Her wish for you is truly to have happiness
Even if and when you make a terrible mess.

Hopefully, before she eclipses the earth
You'll realize her dreams for you began at birth.
Every step you take, and every step you make
She wishes you well for your very own sake.

Every woman giving birth is not a mother
Children to them may be considered a burden
A wise and godly mother trains her babes well.
The whole community can observe and will tell.

Mothers out there, "many eyes are upon you"
A role model must you be and counselor, too.
"Follow Bible teachings, as your constant guide".
Before sunset, it will stimulate your hidden pride.

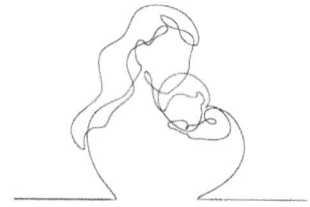

Sisters

Sisters have a special exceptional bond
Their love for each other is mostly fond
They experience each other's hurts
They feel those deep piercing pains.
That expands longer than a midnight train.
When in trouble, in distress or need help
Get to your rescue in a matter of seconds
So quickly you'll wonder who beckoned.
Life so bombarded with major decisions
Sisters will make them turn out virtuous.
My sister, worth a trillion or more dollars,
Never discouraging or putting me down
But uses encouraging words to pick me up
And put me back on that sure solid ground.
Lets me know that it's either right or wrong.
She's wrapped with a huge bow from heaven
With a message, you'll always be my friend,
Clinging together through the thick and thin.
That big bow ties these sisters together forever.
Sister dear, my love for you is immeasurable.

My Big Brother

My big brother is a man of great wisdom
Well versed on a wide variety of subjects
Has traveled wide and near
For God is his greatest fear.

God created my big brother
Specified like no other.
Oh, so tall and handsome
And also pretty awesome.

His beautiful smile
Radiates from a mile.
A talented singer
Plays the strings with his fingers.

An excellent teacher
Don't forget a gospel preacher.
He counsels based on the testaments
Chat with him and observe the evidence.

I am thankful he's been blessed three score ten+
He knows on God's promises, he can depend.
We recognize it was God's Grace that kept him.
Today I say Happy Birthday "Big Brother"
Rev. Dr. Willie J. Short known as "Willie Joe."

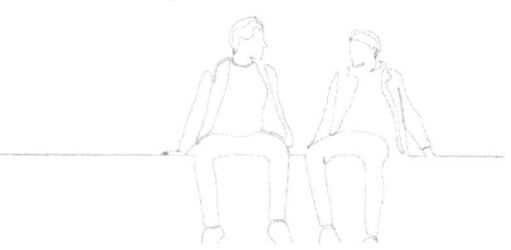

Richard the Grown-Up Baby Brother

My brother kicked in this world in thirty-nine
I can't believe he hates the taste of wine.
He has many ways similar to our daddy
But that beautiful gentle disposition like mommy.

His heart is made of pure gold
His belongings are very hard to hold.
It seems he's always playing Santa Claus
Going around granting wishes for others.

Dad was without transportation, he gave a car
Bringing it from Northern Virginia, right far.
As a child he hung close to our mother
She shared many of life's lessons like no other.

My brother seems to live a lonely life
Cause he doesn't have a caring wife.
His two sisters help bring up the slack
We find his heart needs not hang from a rack.

My Husband

My honey-do is a hell of a man
In any situation he can take a stand.
He fathered two terrific sons with me
Our whole family is grateful to thee.

He looked forward to performing on his job
His love of work causes his heart to throb.
Providing for his beautiful family
Is something he does readily and daily.

Being manly was all he did
For his family, he would roll up his sleeve
Cooking, cleaning, and caring for his children
Earned him an honorary master's degree

My husband has faults, as well all others do
But caring for his family brought him through.
He deserves a merit of honor, tis surely true
His legacy Rondell and John a magnificent outcome.

Rondell And John Jr.

(My Giants)

God graced me with many gifts
Two closest to my heart, my lovely sons
Worth more to me than loads or tons.
They're as different as day is to night.
But values more than any shining Knight.

Rondell, as smart as a genius with potential
Presents himself as shrewd and assertive.
God put him on earth for the role of leader.
He's an individualist who thinks for himself
At times he puts other folk ideas on a shelf
But deep down he sees them standing tall.

John, smart and a great harmonizer
He spreads peace and reframes from harming
His quiet demeanor depicts Godliness.
If he can't help, he will not hinder you.
"Be yourself," society's view of you doesn't matter.
He likes happy people and feels good about self.

God granted my greatest request seeing
My sons educated and caring for themselves.
I am proud of both my sons, and their creation.
PRODUCTIVE CITIZENS! Loving and vivacious.

My Rays of Joy

God's done blessed me real good
He's graced me with two warm-bloods
Kyle and Keane my robust grandsons,
Both of them worth many mega tons.

Kyle my first born to orbit the earth
Easy going, energetic at birth.
Music lover, and enthusiastic student
Learning how to survive, an inspiration.

Keane his brother and the youngest
Loveable, energetic, out-spoken and cleverest
This is my most prized joy, born premature.
Now developed into a knight in shining armor.

These two rays of joy light up my life
My goal lies in keeping them from some strife.
This grandma puts everything aside to help her rays
For the rest of my life, I'll love and cherish their ways.

I won't get enough of their love.

Mirrored Reflection Granddaughters

Granddaughters bring exceedingly great joy
They represent traits of a fine daughter.
God knows how to cause grandparents laughter
I think sometimes they're misused as a play toy.

God granted me the pleasure of two
Lakeisha and Natalie beaming through.
Lakeisha the oldest, deserves all of our love
Natalie so small and fragile soaring like a dove.

I am thankful to God for moments we share
I hope they realize just how much I care.
God is the author and finisher of all things
He is handling obstacles stacked as a bell rings

My granddaughters make me very proud
God's gonna keep us from separating in a cloud
To God be the glory for the blessings we receive
Forget the past, look to the present we must believe.

Karen

God matched me with a unique Goddaughter
Reared by loving, Christian-hearted parents.
Suits my standards and specifications to a T.
She handles herself ladylike constantly.
Uses discretion and serves with dignity
Scholarly, her crest leads to a successful life

My Goddaughter is a blessed well-bread child.
Every time we meet, my fears are calmed
Her actions depicts godly ways and deeds
Her walk is based on family sown seeds
Her talk, Christ-like ordered by her King
Karen lives holy, his calling she'll obey
The adage: a chip off of the old block
Certainly has connection to that solid rock.

A strong, kind and gentle phenomenal lady
I am so proud to be your substitute mother.
To a daughter, I never gave birth to
But, a blissful heart while walking on earth
I pray; the desires of her heart are met and
Extends farther than any of my wildest dreams.

Two Daughters-in-law ? My Inheritance

Let me tell you a thing or two about my two daughters
Hear ye this from someone who works at making it work.
These young ladies so fine, I need a recording clerk
I never ordered them but my young men added them to the family
Like it or not, I can't change it if I wanted to try.

Each is very unique and special in her own way
Creative as a cook, house keeper or at home at a bay.
If my sons can take it who am I to reject it?
My concern is that they look out for my sons' back
And are genuine, cares and careful not to attack.

Both know how to plan and carryout a party
If you have attended one of their functions, lody-dody
You can relax because the pros had hands in that action
Evans/Thompson Coleman/Thompson and company
You'd readily know, no hesitation the in-laws had full control.

Mother-in-law's family gathering incorporates both talents
Lonnice gifted in cooking all sorts of delicious entrees
Belinda is gifted also, but always in place to clean the kitchen
I give both of them A+, they score high with me, that's no lie.
My two daughters-in-law are a blessing to have, I can't deny.

Each is worth more than a ton of gold; they fit well in their mold.
I gladly tell this true story which I shall not let it go untold.

CHAPTER 2

GREEKDOM...

The organization of my heart

That Pink & Green

That Ivy Leaf
&
PEARLS

Especially, Service to all Mankind

The First Black Female
Greek Lettered Sorority

The Place to Be

Aka-land is the place for me
Is it where you want to be?
It provides services to all mankind
With enthusiasm you won't linger behind.

The youth, we'll help become aware
Seniors we can honor because we care.
Inactive Sorors, we can supply your needs
Remember your sisterly vows, and take heed.

Being sisterly, energetic, helpful and powerful,
Leader or follower, we need to work together.
So put AKA back into your HEART
While there is still time to do your part.

Why not keep the vision fair?
That was so nobly begun by a pair.
AKA land is the place for you and me
Designed with grace, integrity and dignity.

Greek Affair

AKA's are lights to the world
Such an array of service they twirl.
No good works for rewards, but for others
AKA's are the salt of the earth
They savor a variety of flavors
Joy is given by our precious maker
Don't fret about man being a caretaker.
Our image, we must not smother
We were first somewhat like a mother.
Let our good work glorify our creator
Our works so Godly and, from the heart
Any other motive is not so smart
We are extraordinary ladies to transform
With extraordinary services to perform
Lights of the community glow for miles
Problems to be solved come in huge files
These ladies love meeting challenges
They are so strong, there's no quitting
Lights so bright they continue emitting.

The Name Dianne . . .

Carries a very nice ring
Being someone with whom to cling.
She leads with dignity and grace
Other Greeks find it a hard act to trace.

She lives up to the high ethical character
Set forth by our Founders as a serious matter.
Raising high her scholastic aptitude
For that, we owe to her a lot of gratitude.

You treat AKA business quite serious
You represent us well in your pink and green attire
You utter words so articulate and eloquently
Your dedication and Charisma are much to be admired

No one ever succeeds without knocks or bruises
Keep in mind you've earned one of AKA's cruises.
With strides and pride you forged ahead
Planning and Serving AKA kept you out of bed.

Congratulations you have served us well
To all of our sorrows we will tell
That our noble founders would be proud, too
Of a phenomenal leader, Dianne Rhoades, that's you.

The Christmas Gift of a Genuine Sister

What a special gift is Christmas
It marks the birth of the Christ Child
A time when sisters demonstrate a oneness
Which was part of the pledge that we made.

Celebrating Christmas has a special reason
And it arrives in a very unique season.
Just like that time when we were made sisters
Everyone else was excluded, even the misters.
What better joyous time to share and reminisce?

God created each of us in his own image
He even loves us with an unconditional love
His love must be shared through us for all
Genuine sorors emulate love such as Christ's.
At Christmastime, especially when it's activated.

Mediating on the true meaning of Christmas
Renewing of our vows as genuine sorrows
There is a distinct connection between the two.
Let's take this Christmas to spark a relationship
Similar to the one such as the one we have with Jesus.

What a special gift, too are wonderful people
Like you All my precious jewels SORORS
May LOVE-JOY-PEACE-HAPPINESS remain
Yours to have this Holiday season and for evermore.

In order to receive love, you must give love.
There is a reason for the season as well as a genuine sisterhood.

The Miraculous Eight Pearls

Each of you should take flight
To join selective ladies of great insight
In rendering service to all mankind
We do this with great delight.

There is a strong bond in the land
In which others may not have a hand
We work together like no other
Implementing worldwide each program strand.

Miraculous eight, you must take a stand
To render service as one strong band
Committed and involved in service projects
As the wiles of the world, we withstand.

We share such valuable resources
As we strive to choose our courses
We ask our ladies to be reserved
As they overcome opposing forces.

Keep AKA standards high
They must never be laid by
As we hold high the torch
Our scholarly attributes, we must not deny.

December 16, 2001

Sharon's Bundle of Joy

Baby, Baby cute and cuddly
Who's the fairest of them all?
A shining star before you're born
Evidenced by tooting horns.

Everyone extends much love to you
Before you enter into this world.
You'll be praised by thriving poets,
Photographed by family and friends.

Newborns are completely helpless,
A cheerful environment erases restlessness
A lovely, caring surrounding, a reality
For the development of a healthy
personality.

Baby requires much love and affection
Precious AKA Sisters, my prescription
Do you ladies hear what I hear?
Attention ladies "I'm an AKA girl."

Golden Girls: Our Legacy

Golden Sorors are precious jewels
A wealth of knowledge they impart
Delivered straight from the heart
My, they'll keep you refueled.

Dedicated, thoughtful and wise
Those golden girls are hard to find
Sophisticated and one of-a kind
Standing tall without compromise.

Bravo! Kudos! Accolades! Sorors
No greater "Love" has any Greeks
Than your "Sisters" have for you
Priceless gems, sincere and rare,
Far, far beyond compare.

Sisters by Heart

Life is a building, so is our sisterhood
It rises slowly day-by-day.
Every new lesson we learn may
Lay a block that will forever stay.
Every experience adds to our clock.
Every touch of another life in ours
Strengthens the bond of sisterhood and
Alpha Kappa Alpha power.
Every influence that impresses us
Should be blessings as beautiful as flowers
For you it's just the beginning
We are now Sisters by Heart . . .
We'll share so much laughter
And bear each other's tears
Our spiritual kinship
Will grow stronger each year.
We're not sisters by birth
But we've known from the start
God put us together to be Sisters by Heart.

Two Great Women of Substance

Let me enlightening you about two courageous giants
One is Corretta King who worked hard for women rights.
The other is Rosa Parks who shared some important remarks.
Both of whom we can say were influential near college park.

Rosa Parks stirred up a great big fuss
Refusing to give up her seat on a bus.
Front row seats were for whites only
Rosa became tired of this situation
As a result she was jailed and lost her job
And opened to many racial insults
Rosa's sacrifices were well worth the results.
Her situation brought on the civil right movement.

Corretta King is known as the Civil rights activist
Behind her husband's death she perpetuated his ideals.
Recognized for keeping Dr. King's dream alive
Very soon after his assassination she took a big dive.
As a dynamic activist and peace crusader
Working on women rights and problems they faced
Because of Corretta, we can conclude she brought no disgrace.

Two courageous, strong and brave giants
Who worked hard to weather many storms
In order that the world and sisters live in dignity
Women of respect and integrity were inducted into our sorority.

CHAPTER 3

LIFE'S DEFINING MOMENTS AS THINGS CHANGE

Our Rose

Knowing that your steps are ordered by God
The Pastor's Aide of this great church
Sought out to make some of your steps easier
Our responsibility is to serve as your right hand.

We stepped here and there, near and far, too
To prepare a bag of necessities just for you
Whereas this kind gesture freed up more time
Your sermons show, your time has been well spent.

We pondered at things we can do to assist you
So, we have some handkerchiefs to dry your eyes
Sometimes you know not what they are for
One thing, for sure is they are either for sorrow or joy.

Lotion to soften your hand for anointing
Clear lip balm to moisten your lips for preaching.
A picture key chain with Jesus, a reminder of his teaching
Armored in the proper gear will keep us from disappointing.

God, an encourager, and counselor, orders our steps
Lawanda Adams say, no matter what you are going through
God is using you, Cause "The battle is not yours, it's the Lord's
Rev. Spencer, the Pastor Aide members give you a big applaud.

Boys

Boys, Boys, they are mostly all right
Assign tasks, won't make them uptight.
Snakes, snails and puppy dog tails
Good for running long rocky trails.
Built to do hard and strenuous work.

Strong, robust so my mysteriously wise
Solve problems or mess them up.
Kiss little girls and make them cry
Hard to calm, regardless of how you try
Adventurous, energetic, and experimental.

Helpful in creating more of their kind
The population will never lag behind.
Girls think boys are some kind a fine
Question them, they surely will whine.
Proud boys, they are full of themselves.

Eleventh of September

A day that saddened my heart to know
People would stoop so extremely low
To interrupt a nation's daily operation.
Taking so many many innocent lives.
Separating hosts of families just won't jive.
Each of us experienced a terrible blow.

Efforts are made to discover reasons why
Masterminds are still profoundly baffled
Because many were caught off guard
Effectual prayer is where we turned
Respect for God we must adhere to
A wake-up call has peeped through.

Terrorists and Americans all, we shall
Be sentenced by God, a secret judge
His commandments state the penalty.
I certainly am glad it wasn't me.
God is still in charge and always will be.
He is King of Kings and Lord over all.

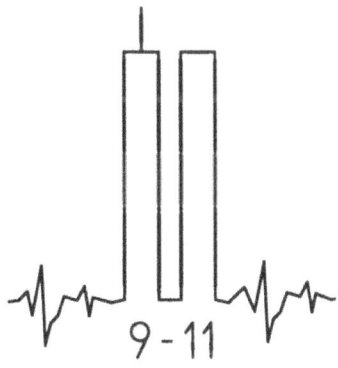

That Special Friend

I have a friend, unique and like no other
I can share my innermost secrets,
No one else will ever, ever know.
I can ask for help and advice at all times,
This friend is always waiting for me there.
When I need comfort and assurance or
Desire quietness or peace of mind,
In trials and tribulations he's certainly kind.
I couldn't seek nor find no better friend.

The love for me is true and unconditional,
Love is there to share no matter what.
I am unable to see, taste, hear and touch
But, that omnipresent spirit enfolds me
It is worth more to me than gems and gold.

This friend is none other than my creator
My lawyer, burden bearer, doctor and director
If you are not acquainted with this friend
You are missing more than you will ever realize.
That friend is none other than Jesus Christ.

Senior Citizens

Store a WEALTH of indispensable history
That's very important to a family's LEGACY
A senior citizen is SEASONED with KNOWLEDGE,
OPINIONS weigh tons because of various EXPERIENCES.
TOUCH upon so many aspects on life's journey
Save and PROTECT many people from strife.
It is they who have faced many obstacles in life
ENCOURAGING words uttered brightens the future
ADVICE is worth more than diamonds and pearls
Worthy of shouting a recitation in Shay Stadium
Their INTUITION signals warnings to be heeded,
Saving other citizens from problems seeded.
VALUES are built on sound religious principles
God's word, is the only GUIDE for their instructions,
Directing them to travel paths in the RIGHT direction.
For, they are so deserving of any honor given you.
The Master's plan allowed them to reach this ripe AGE,
Cause they are needed to connect each link in life's chain
Seeing is believing," they're an EXAMPLE for young and old"
We commend and salute you for your WISDOM shared.

The Beauty in My Beautician

My beautician lives up to her name
The way she lives life is truly a beauty.
Aside from performing occupational tasks
She involves herself with the whole customer.

My beautician's name is Mary Naomi
This lady is so caring and very kind
Shows concern for more than lovely hair
She makes sure you're comfortable in her chair.

When customers are burdened with despair
My beautician, Naomi is always there.
If someone dies or has an event, she bakes a cake
I am thankful, Naomi can fix hair and also bake.

My beautician does all of these wonderful things
She loves God and to others love she brings
I am so grateful this lady takes care of my hair
She's a blessed connection to have that's rare.

To some beauty deals with physical Attraction
An attribute of good looks or loveliness
For me beauty deals with blessedness

My Colleagues

I gave one half of my life to education
Many relationships evolved.
Some of you have been there for me
I might have been as an encourager,
It might have been as a helper,
And perhaps even an inspirer
Whatever the contribution, I say
"Thank You" and I appreciate it all.
Whether it was something great or
As tiny as a morsel, You have been
The wind beneath my wings.
With the help of God, who strengthens me?
And your nurturing that enhances me
This proud, dedicated, open-minded teacher
Has been touched and pass the torch to others.
Favorable imprints remain for generations.
The race is not given to the swift but to
Him who endureth until the end wins.
"I have won my race, but not alone"
I have my colleagues to be thankful for.

Church

Some people consider church a structure
I truly believe it is the people there
Who spill the anointing spirit in the air.

The environment is sacred and solemn
Folk are respectful and reverence God,
The source from which blessings flow
So enormous, you can't help but glow.

Carry something to church with you
Heavy weights can be left there, too.
By no means do you bring them back
Meditation should not attention lack.

Open up and allow God full control
Anchored in God and steadily unfold
Determine your ultimate destination.
Members, responsible for their own salvation.

Now, watch how the church will be blessed
God's word is sufficient and only teacher
Motivated by an anointed spirited preacher.

Books

Books may be read for leisure
On land or sea can bring pleasure.
Knowledge gained is of great benefit
And save your life in unseen danger.

Fascinating they pose a challenge
Because of information gathered.
Imaginative you create the scene
As thought of in a wild or weird dream.

Beautiful; however all aren't easy reading
Lessons they teach last a lifetime worth believing.
Many books are not worth a dime
I love books creating laughter, certainly no crime.

From a library books may be borrowed
Take care of them and read until tomorrow
The choice lies with you as to the color or subject
Examining the contents is the purpose or object.

Children

Children are a gift from God
God commands us to spare not the rod.
It is important that we raise them with love
Depending on God' guidance from above.

Let us care for our children at home
So we won't have to worry about them in Rome.
Allow them to be children when they are young
If you don't they are going to prove you wrong.

Children can be compared to Kites
They were created to fly
But they need a lot of strong wind
Leaving lots of chances for them to bend.

A child raised in a Christian family
Displays becoming behavior daily.
A child will not fall far from its block
For they are surely watched as hands on a clock

My Neck

Oh! My horrible hurting neck
It feels as if it's going to break.
I never imagined such pain
Misery emerges before the rain.
Searching for a comfortable place to lie
If not found soon, I believe I'll die.

Every little move I make
Others can observe it in my shake.
I chat consistently with my creator
Every day, all day I need this director.
The past two days the misery increased
From this day and on, it must decrease.

Thanks to Bengay, most often used
Assisted me to this point without abuse,
And with doses of Celebrex medication
I soon fell on my knees in celebration
With a thankful heart for near recovery
The bittersweet lingers in my memory.

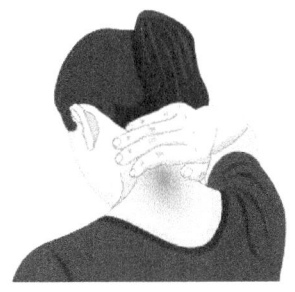

Youth

Enjoy life as early during your youth
Thinking before you run off at the mouth.
They bring many creative ideas into play
Some if which can spoil a good day.
Adult guidance and advice will correct
Saving youth from self destruction
God created these adorable jewels
Growing up for many is a complicated thing.
Harmones have them doing things weird
Like growing a long grayish beard.
Making decisions not thought through
Like putting education on the back burner too.
We must not write them off, nor put them down
Cause they need our direct attention for maturity.

The Effects of Change

Summer fun is rushed out
While fall reaping comes about
Harvest time is nearly at hand
Yielding foods from fertile land.

New growth is the emerging trend
As changes in nature begin to blend
Grass starts turning dingy brown
For a new season's coming to town.

Autumn leaves, an array of colors beautify
Swaying trees giving reasons to testify.
Sweet potatoes peep out of fertile dirt
Collard greens hit by frost won't hurt.

Changing seasons, harm some folk
A runny nose for others isn't a joke.
A change of season has to be
To satisfy every need provided by thee.

Change is effective and necessary
To make way for winter in January
Just when you think it is all over
'Tis almost time to hunt for a four-leaf clover.

Changes come in and changes go out
So many changes make you holler and shout.
Seasonal changes give humans a choice to make.
As for me all are great, but spring I'll gladly take.

I want to be like Dr. King

I want to be just like Dr. King
Seeing to it that freedom rings.
He wasn't about as life of violence
Which often required refrain and silence.

How marvelous this world would be
If we stand at times planted like a tree
We should be proud of his successful mission
Before completing it, he saw it in a vision

Yes, I want to be just like Dr. Martin L. King
Who showed the whole wide world
Blocked out ugly words and actions often hurled
Cherish his memory in the wind beneath my wings

I want to be just like Dr. King
Sacrificed his life that others may live
Was a mighty noble and generous gift
I'd ponder over moving towards that shift

Dr. King, I admire and view as a role model
Many of his qualities were instilled as a toddler
Americans open your eyes, taste and see
That it was a good movement, for eternity.

His dream was put in first gear that year
For, those of us left behind to continually revere.

CHAPTER 4

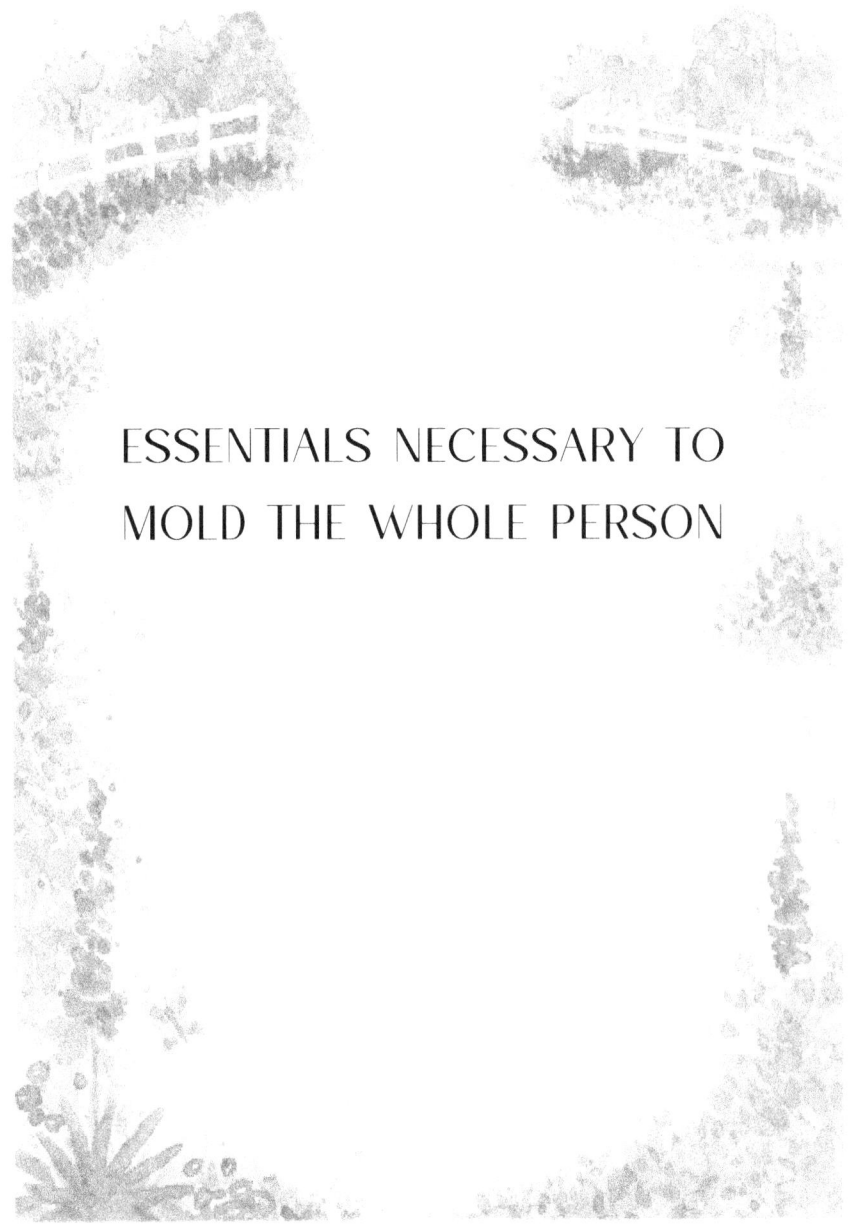

ESSENTIALS NECESSARY TO MOLD THE WHOLE PERSON

My Friend Thomasine
Friends are the flowers that bloom in life's garden.

Thomasine, she's my close friend
We've been through thick and thin
Our relationship has no end.

We go way back, into the sixties
When we took education as a challenge
We shared several things in common

Mature adults, family oriented with a purpose
We served as role models for young adults.
Believe it or not, they listened and looked up to us.

We made it, touched many lives and now retired.
To God be the glory for the things he has done
Friends, we've been for thirty-six wonderful years.
There isn't anything I would not do for Thomasine

She is always welcome in my home, forever will be
And she certainly made me feel welcomed in hers.

Thomasine is thoughtful, trustworthy
Honest, humble
Outstanding, Open-minded
Meek, Miraculous
Ambitious, Admirable
Sincere, Steadfast
Intelligent, Inspirational
Noble, Enthusiastic, Energetic

WHAT A BLESSING IT IS THAT OUR PATHS CROSSED.
ACCOLADES TO MY BEST FRIEND.

Virginia

My role model, Soror and friend
Named for our state "for lovers"
She wears this name very well
Her presence causes vibrations on a bell

Her kindness over runs deeply
Experience it and be touched.
It will make you act in ways positively
This lady is respected and respects others daily.

Virginia nicknamed "Mother of presidents".
First four of five were from this state.
This says a lot for this special lady
She ranks in the top with a celebrity

Virginia stands tall in her undertakings
She does it right or none at all.
So knowledgeable and knows where it's found
Scrabble playing heightens her words every round

Its seal displays the Roman Goddess of eternity
As Virginia's expertise values greatly in quality
When I call, my friend answers with sincerity
I'm thankful to Virginia for enhancing my poetry

In my world Guinness book of life's stand-out
This giant stands tall in an astronomical amount.

African-American Women in History

A woman's **commitment** is first to the home
Often times **she does** things for herself when all alone.
We have some **energetic** women and all are so strong
They will never intentionally **lead** anyone wrong.

Honorary member and "First Lady of Song," a champ
Ella Fitzgerald, honored on a Black Heritage Stamp
An authentic Trailblazer depicting Alpha Kappa Alpha ideals
Her voice and music were so surreal

Marian Anderson, the world's greatest Contralto
Probed very deep for words singing alto
She contended with a considerable amount of discrimination
But to perform on Lincoln Memorial steps showed determination.

Gwendolyn Brooks has a story she certainly had to tell
She represented children in her body of works well
Because of her color she had no need to be ashamed
Cause she was inducted in the Hall of Fame

Another such person in poetry to know is **Maya Angelou**
Who was the first black streetcar conductor in San Francisco
And when she found her voice, speaking was her choice
As she recited her poem at Clinton's Inauguration, we did rejoice.

Bessie Coleman, first woman to earn a pilots license in aviation
Denied training on United States soil due to discrimination
To Europe she went and earned a local and international permit
Died before establishing a school for blacks, that would have been a hit

Mae Jemison's pursuit in space travel came to fruition
When elevated by National Aeronautic Administration.
First African American woman astronaut, to fly into space
A week orbiting Earth on space shuttle Endeavor was her place.

A Prayer of Thankfulness

Thank you God for this valuable book
Many drew history from their nook.
Thank you for our gracious leader, Jean
Who led and directed our blessed team.

Every Tuesday the Committee gathered
Where opinions and ideas really mattered.
Talented members from various churches
Collected, arranged and made lots of purchases.

Thanks for traveling mercies you bestowed
Fellowship that existed in this you blessed
The hours you allowed us were well spent
Even though there were times we had to repent.

We worked hard and with love to obtain unity
In the quaint little LaCrosse Community
Which brought together the RZUA Journal.
To God be the glory for the wonderful things he's done.

Share our legacy; be well informed as you read
And know that you are a big part of the Universal Church.
THE CHURCH OF ZION THE CHURCH OF GOD.

(May 24, 2005)

Family Trip

A trip planned, God in the forefront
Works well every single time
His loving arms present for protection
His eyes piercing through in all directions
We release to him all of our concerns or cares.

Four hundred miles, a break at Shoney's
The service was superb and food so tasty.
Such large portions, we were wasteful
Our stomachs so crammed couldn't take it.
We acknowledge God for blessing every bit.

We awoke in Comfort early from a restful night.
It was his grace that blessed our sight.
A Continental Breakfast superb to our delight
Blessings in abundance started the next flight.
Approaching Jacksonville, now riding high.

God's mercy, he blessed and kept us safe
No! We won't let go no-no-no-no-no-o-o
Observing his goodness, palm trees appear.
Several bodies of water, so deep and clear.
Nearing our destination, the big rain begins.

Journey complete all safe and in His hands.

February

A significant Month

The second month of the calendar year
So loaded with magnificent events
Birthdates of famous presidents
Ground hog day and Afro-American month
But greatest of all recognitions for Blacks.

To begin with the aforementioned is not right
Every day should tell of Blacks' plights.
Why isn't this so or even a hassle or fight?
They are just as deserving as anyone else
Its high time we bring closure to a lengthy myth.

This month signifies unconditional love
Whether you are for change, or against a move.
Beware of Gods commandments which warns us
What we must do to reach our journey's end
Brighten the spot where you are, from now til then.

February arrives just prior to Spring in March
When flowers bloom and gives rise to new life
So many people wed at this time, adding a wife.
Check out your life's history to see how you fit
I guarantee there is some connection that hit.

A Woman

(Folio No. P3168482)

A woman has a tremendous job to do
She has to be strong also loving to make it through.
For her husband, she's his help mate and
For her children a role model and nurturer, too
When depressed a woman can brighten any day.

Need a shoulder to cry on a woman has two of the best
In need of advice a woman will share from her little nest.
Scared or afraid a woman will stand by your side
Need a helping hand a woman will not refuse the ride.
Whatever the need a woman is at your beckoning call.

A woman binds wounds and mends breaks
While others in the world seemingly forsakes.
She is someone with that unconditional love
A woman is then, second to the Creator above.
When you need to talk, a woman will sit to listen.

God equipped woman with lots of miraculous skills
Her commitment to the family's well-being thrills.
A woman takes more than her share to avoid strife
Rears her children by living the example like a good wife.
A Christian woman has faith, she preservers and is patient.

Yearly Celebration

To little sister's house

From big brother's house.
Each year we share something special
So thankful, we survived to made it through.
Blessed with so many wonderful things
Thankful cause we know not what the future brings
Greetings for family, close friends and acquaintances
Updated on accomplishments, sadness and successes
This annual gang has developed a unique bond
Twenty some years the relationships have grown fond.
Everyone looking forward to Martha's good cooking
The whole gang travels near and far just a looking.
All of those decorative and beautiful veggie dishes
A variety of delicious home-cooked assorted desserts
Wow! Don't mention the tenderized tasty meats
Whipped up into delectable gourmet treats.
Anyone missing the Jones, Thompson celebration
Will have to catch us for our next year's creation
Which will have us travel to our designated place
With southern-hospitality-dinner prepared by Grace.

Who Are Your Friends?

The extent of a true friend is immeasurable
For the eyes see without fault
All criticisms are made discreetly
A friend won't tell you what you want to hear
But that which needs to be said.
Everything said and done leads to growth
Addressing things that are most needed
For friends' blessings are never-ending.
Friends are with you in sunshine and rain,
Friends are with you in pleasure and pain,
In losses or gains, always there in all ways.
Their love is unconditional and lasting.
One door always open to you, a friend's
Choose carefully whom you befriend.
Helen Steiner Rice says it well-
The more of everything you share
The more you'll always have to spare
The more you love, the more you'll find
That life is good and friends are kind.

Do you know who your friends are?

CHAPTER 5
TRIBUTES TO INSPIRATIONAL LEADERS

"Inspiration comes to us slowly and quietly...prime it with a little solitude"

Our Bishop

George Hammett Studivant is his name
He is not about playing any game.
He is one of God's chosen servants
Under his anointing, motivated by the Holy Spirit
Certainly, he knows the value of daily prayer.

A man of good character and many kind deeds
His faith, much more than the grains of mustard seeds.
When his life seems empty with nowhere to go
When his heart becomes troubled and his spirit low
There's a glow in his face because . . .

He knows to turn, always to God
He learned to trust Him who is all-powerful
When friends are few and nobody cares
He knows who hears him every hour
He knows he'll be carried on the wings of love.

Bishop has been charged with leading a flock
Using understanding and wisdom he is strong as a rock.
He prepares as he gets lost in meditation
To bring people life-changing inspiration
As he is led by God through the rain and storm.

This extraordinary Bishop is anchored in the Lord
He believes his promises and follows his plan
God eliminates earthly troubles and gives him peace
God gives him strength to face and finish life's daily tasks.
Bishop has learned that God's good grace is sufficient and
He will never fail nor leave him alone.

Anna

Ambitious

Negotiator

Navigator

Apologetic

Working hard trying to make things click
Having God in her corner, her pick
You must consider carefully all things
However, children to Christ you try to bring.
Anna is always planning special events
Inviting youth to take an active part
Of God's program at an early start.
She roams around in the community
Encouraging youth to show dignity.
Sister, as long as you know in your heart
You're working on kingdom building
All of your efforts will not go unnoticed.
With God beside you and holding your back
Your everything else gives rise to new life.
As you say it," You are the Bishop's wife."

A Salute In Appreciation For Many Years Of Service

I-Isaac is a man of integrity and great character
S-Served as Keeper of Finances for many years
A-A man that has been dedicated to this job
A-A mild-mannered man who is dependable
C-Commitment, a trait that fits him very well.

C-Coleman values his job that he solicited help
O-Only from his expert son in the accounting field
L-Loves the Lord, his church and his family.
E-Efficient in executing his assigned responsibilities
M-Manages the finances of the RZUA Churches
A-Appreciation is quite modest for such a man of
His caliber. "A Giant" whose shoulders we stand.
N-Never too busy to do an outstanding job.

**Deacon Isaac Coleman we join others in Saying,
"You've served us well for years."**

A Tribute

A tribute to a mom, sister, aunt and worker in the community
You'll find her working in peace and dignity
Mrs. Ruby Short, a lady of high standards
Not so high that she forgets her service to mankind.
She gives of herself and time unselfishly
She uses the graces empowered by God alone
Kindness, goodness and faithfulness
To ensure a working relationship in trying times.

God created Mrs. Ruby Short to his own liking
He equipped her with tools for leading.
It was a creator's plan that she serve at this center.
She has made a difference in so many ways
She has been a beacon of light to some
A ray of joy to others
A bucket filled with hope for another
And an inspiration to all.
Her presence is felt all over this place
It matters not what color the face.

YOUR FAMILY, FRIENDS AND CHURCH FAMILY
Join the Senior Citizens in saying, "we value your work."
Thanks for a job well done, we love you and
Appreciate all that you do, have done and will continue to do.
God Bless You

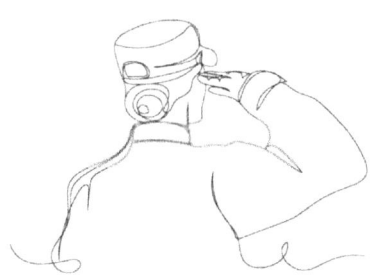

Cleo Conscientious

Likable

Efficient

Open-minded

Cleo is a hard working soul
In Greensville County, she played her role.
Her dedication Immeasurable
Association with her has been pleasurable.
She mapped out her action-plan very well
Just watch the outcome and you can tell.
Cleo got the job done with a team or alone
Her success must be recorded on the heavenly throne.
She touched the lives of students using special tool
In the home, church, community and school
She taught them everything from A to Z
So productive citizens they will be.

As you RETIRE from your occupation
Think of it as going on a daily vacation.
Thirty-three years you've done your best
To prepare your students for passing the test
No more lesson plans to prepare each night
Charting your course will be your right.
Excellence was always your intent
We applaud you for a career well spent.
So put away those lesson plans and SOL tests
And enjoy many years of peaceful rest.
Goodwyn, your last name, says it all
For you have mastered a lot of good wins.

A Tribute To Our Presidents

Three energetic presidents-Barbara, Juanita and Melvin Drew
Realizing the tremendous task they accepted to do
Rolled up their sleeves and vowed not to shirk
As they set out to do their assigned work.

Back in their respective chapters, the fun really started
For information to members had to be imparted
And ideas and input were solicited from each member
On how to complete everything by the last of December.

The goal in mind is to lead their chapter in coming together as one
To distribute the multitude of duties and tasks that must be done
In order to be ready for the BIG ALUMNI MEETING date.
Which the National President said could not be late.

If you think the job of these leaders has been easy and slow
Here's something you surely need to know
Challenges and letdowns, they would often meet
But they wouldn't give in to "Mr. Defeat."

A leader is nothing without followers loyal and true
Followers must know what they are expected to do
Out three presidents each worked with zeal
To keep the Mid-Winter Conference alive and real.

So hats off to Barbara, Juanita and Drew
We sincerely thank you for all you do
To serve as leaders with greatest resolve
That Brunswick, Greenville, and Mecklenburg
Chapters will always be involved.

The Fragrance of a Virtuous Woman

(Mrs. Gertrude H. Peterson)

Mrs. Gertrude as we called her
Left a wonderful fragrant behind.
A fruit of the Spirit she manifests, kindness
Always had encouraging words to share,
Always did things that showed she cared.
Her love was unconditional and lots of it to spare.
Meek and humble was she?
Her main objective was to live for thee.
Her guidance, was always welcomed
From the people of her surroundings.
She lived abundantly, and gave others lavishly
Her acts of kindness were unselfish.
She made others very happy and was happy, too.
Its people like Mrs. Gertrude who
Makes the world a wonderful place
By doing the things that she did-
A genuine smile, kind, thoughtful deeds or
A hand outstretched in an hour of need.
Flowers leave their fragrance on
The hand that bestow them.

That sums up the life of our friend and
lovely neighbor. Her fragrance remains with
the many of us whose lives she has touched.

Tribute To Elected Officials

Hear Ye! Hear Ye! Brunswickians and neighbors
We've come to celebrate a phenomenal event
Changes have been made to a governing board
For this reason we recognize all elected officials.

Entrusted to you the responsibilities are great
Your position wasn't given because of any fate
The citizens saw something unique in you
It's up to you to let your something shine through

We will observe how you speak on our behalf
The way you stand up and represent the people
We have the confidence that you will do what's right
That which will benefit the whole community

Watch, pray for man who may work to decrease
Always remember God gives the increase
Ask God to guide you and order your steps
As you make decisions that will, the community, help.

You can count on us, just you wait and see
God bless you as you face many adversities
Claim victory for God has charted your course
Serve faithfully, be honest, and stay focused and committed.

We salute and recognize you today.

A Tribute To . . .

Reverend Ina B. Owens

Lna B. Owens often called "Bell"
Noted for sharing candy canes
Acclaims the gospel of Jesus Christ.

Ordained minister of RZUA Churches
Worships God with all her heart
Endeavors to promote unity and teamwork
Nurtures the precious name of Jesus.
Serves the Lord with gladness daily.

Reverend Owens is a caring and giving person
She loves the Lord and passes love to others
She is appreciative of all of her blessings
And in return she blesses other loved ones.
Reverend Owens is a child of the King in sincerity.

She possesses qualities emulating those of Christ
Kindness, loving, meekness, peaceful and helpful.

Jesus loves a cheerful giver
And
That means you and me and all of his children.

A Tribute In Memory of Deceased

Members (2001- 2006)
Of
Ogden Chapel Presbyterian Church

Today we celebrate Homecoming
Let's not forget members gone home.
Soldiers who labored in the vineyard
They worked diligently and mighty hard.
Trying to make the journey worthwhile.

Certainly The Lord uses ordinary people
And he equips them for specific tasks.
Each member gone on performed very well
Listen attentively everyone to the story we tell.
As we meditate on each that is listed by name

Bettie Hawkins Feggans, the youngest of them all
In service to the Sunday and Bible School stood very, very
tall.

Martin Short, a member of the Pastors' Aide
Saw to it that the minister's comfort was always made.

Leater Gholson sang sweet melodies in the choir
Enhanced the worship service with her soft voice.

Agnes Gates served many years as Church Clerk
Willingly and efficiently she carried out her work.

Esther Green played the piano with vim
As she provided music to various hymns.

Robert Bruce not only assisted in building the church
But, speaking on its behalf was part of his work

William "Pat" Hawkins aided in building the Church
His dependability was necessary for construction to work.

Robert Penn was also dedicated to the church's creation
Especially instrumental in pouring its foundation.

They all have fulfilled the Master's Plan
He's called them home to the Promised Land
You are home where you can rest
He makes no mistakes, He only takes the best.

"2006"

Seasoned Citizens

Senior citizens are Gods gift
To the maturing youth adults and all
They've been to many faraway places
Observed many faces
And know how to direct, guide and advise.

How do they know these things?
Taught by valuable lessons based on
Knowledge, experience, serious encounters
Trials, tribulations and hardships that
Forced them to connect in a divine relationship

They have learned, no questions asked
For it was Almighty God who blessed
Just take a look around this room
They have the activity of their limbs
Beautiful silky, gray accented hair trim

Your expertise is prestigious and essential
You of all people can discern the adversary
Experience your teacher to handle situations
"Never feel worthless because you are needed."

Some generations think they know everything
You have lived your life three scores plus some
There's no question on what you can offer
Seeing is believing cause you've witnessed
The fulfillment in the Holy Bible

I love you. Adore and honor you
Our Golden Citizens

Precious Previous Published Poetry

By

International Library of Poetry

Songs of Honour	"A Woman"
The Sound of Poetry	"My Neck"
A Moment in Eden	"21st Century Scholars"
3-CD Collection	"I Want to Be Like Dr. King"
Theatre of the Mind	"My Colleagues"
The Colors of Life	"My Inspirational Leader"

The best poems and best poets 2005
"Volunteering"

The Best Poems and Best Poets 2001-2002
"Life"

My poems printed above have been included in the publications as copyrighted compilation which remains my property. My VIP P3168482 International Library of Poetry (poetry.com)

A TRIBUTE TO RUTH S. PHILLPS

Mrs. Ruth Phillips is a most kind and special lady
Referred to as "Ma Phillips" by SPC students
Her life's calling is Queen of culinary beauty
She considers no short cuts to her involved duty.

Creatively and talented she assumes each task.
Be assured it's professional and fit for a King
Her traits are taken from the Fruit of the Spirit
A lady of goodness, faithfulness and of merit.

Her southern style food is flavored to perfection
The décor complements the setting with distinction.
A lady of few words, yet firm and with authority
Hats off to "Ma Phillips," a beacon in this community.

Virdie Merritt
A Woman of God

Anyone walking in God's way
Deserves accolades that say
I'm living daily for a heart like God's
I am nothing without Him
With and through Him all things are possible.

She shows love for her fellowman
She keeps her hand in his hand.
She knows that without Him
The road would be mighty dim
Cause can't nobody do you like Jesus.

A woman meek and humble
Will not allow herself to stumble.
She's anchored in God who strengthens
Because of her obedience, her days are lengthened
May God continue to provide for her every need

Rev. Virdie Merritt be blessed
One of the first women ministers ordained
In the RZUA Churches of America
We proudly honor you with distinction.
"One of God's Chosen Leaders"

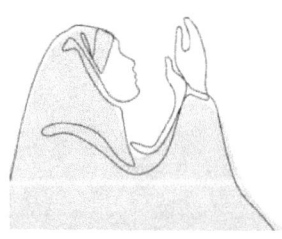

A Tribute to Miss Lisa Owens, Ph.D.

September 1, 2001

Lisa, the scholar as envisioned by this proud teacher
Intelligent, splendid and endowed with integrity
Shining in smiles that radiates and strikes others
Achiever as demonstrated by the degree she holds

Outstanding scholar, knowledgeable and shows it too
Wise, full of wisdom that's mixed with understanding
Ethical character flavored with good sound judgement
Noble enough for the World Guinness Book of Records

I salute you today for a job well done and preservance
Enough to continue growing, growing, growing.

A Tribute to Teachers / Support

TEACHERS, you are very special
You mold, share and change lives
You move mountains
You touch the Future and
Shape the minds of our leadership
In the nation.
You're unsung heroes.

The word appreciation
Is a small word
When you sum up the "Day" of a teacher
And if it were not for ESP
To cut down some of your steps
What would you do?

We appreciate you first, as colleagues
And encourage you to teach as unto
The supernatural powers that worketh in you.

We appreciate you and all you do.

My Inspirational Leader

A man after God's heart
Affording me the VERY same start
He saw in me what I did not
He chose me to advise our youth
Giving lessons to live on OF TRUTH

Sunday after Sunday I prepared
Messages motivated by the Holy Spirit
Guided by my relationship with God
My Doctor said I would never again talk
I was encouraged to take a closer walk

We both proved the devil IS a liar
Cause God is in charge of our lives
Thanks to Rev. Alvin B. Thomas, MY LEADER
I'm a soldier still living for Jesus DAILY
I am determined to emulate his own heart

You have touched so many lives
Your God-given gift and DEVOTION
Your love for the Lord shows all over
It certainly spreaded and caught hold of me

I am no longer the same person because
my inspirational leader taught me well.

Twenty-First Century Scholar

Having earned the name 21ˢᵗ Century Scholar
It is really a hard act to follow
It will give others a run for the dollar
Time was well-spent on academics
And worth pursuing for your education
It certainly will determine your occupation.

Soar like eagles to reach the moutaintop
"You" are viewed as the cream of the crop
Your expertise will be valued and sought quite a lot
That is why you must persist
A lot of critical thinking is required
Your scholarly attributes are much to be desired.

The sophisticated ladies of AKA
Are truly happy, to salute you here today
Because of your wise academic way
Your scholarly attribute, your priority
Is the reason you're honored by this great sorority.

GODMOTHER

(written by God-Daughter Karen Swann)

When you need someone
to talk to
I hope you will
talk to me

When you need someone
to laugh with
I hope you will
laugh with me

When you need someone
for advice
I hope you will
turn to me

When you need someone
to help you
I hope you will
let me help you

I cherish and love
everything about you
And I will always support you
as a goddaughter, as a person
and as a friend

For the Extraordinary Teacher

(written by Lisa Owen)

An ordinary teacher?
Maybe so to anyone
Who's never been calmed by her smile that
breaks out just like the morning sun
Or never heard her talking
in that voice so rich and clear
Or never sat down in her classroom, for a lesson on life.

An ordinary teacher?
Maybe so to someone who
has never been a witness
To the good works she can do
or never gotten all wrapped up
Inside one of her stories that
Make the difficult, easy; the must be done,
an I want to do; and the unpleasant, a pleasure.

An ordinary teacher?
Maybe so to someone who
has never been forgotten, dismissed, or pigeon holed
And then been rescued by her just speaking
the words "I believe in you!"

An ordinary teacher?
No!
To all the people that her life
has touched-and there's a lot-
An ordinary teacher
is exactly what she is not!

In memory of Deceased Classmates

In a class totaling 125, our lives speak distinctly for us
And the plan of our creator allows three score plus.
We know not the minute, nor the hour we'll leave the place we reside
But our belief in salvation determines where we abide
Though a few of our classmates have terminated

The memories linger, unabated
Footprints embedded on the wall
Shows their account, as they answered the call

God created each of us in his own image to tell his story
With talent to use for His honor and glory
Some excelled in sports, to name a few:
Thelma, Edith, Howard, Claude, and Shirley Harrison, too
Robert, Glorice, Cynthia and Ada also made their sports debut

A few he anointed for the ministry of musical instruments and song
Lawrence, Chester, Nelson, James, and Mamie were among
Emma and Rose all were melodious in a very celestial way
With Lawrence, Chester, Nelson, and James singing around heaven
all day.

The rest of our classmates he used for his glory
This multitude he empowered to tell his story.
Louise, Joseph, Juanita, Ella, Kennneth and Virginia
Shirley, Earl, Joe, Frank , Frederick, Adria, and Lucinda

In their heavenly home they took their stand
They are all together in God"s Christian band.
As they sing praises to God above
We miss them at our 5oth reunion and each of them we love.

POEM WRITTEN ON THE 50TH CLASS REUNION, IN
MEMORY OF DECEASED MEMBERS OF THE 1959 CLASS.

CHAPTER 6
Soul Soothing Writing I did in the Pandemic

Eleven years have passed since the first edition of Expressions Sanctioned by God Through the Eyes of Amazing Grace was published. WHAT HAS CHANGED?

A virus rushed in caught everyone off guard. A pandemic that no one has seen before has the experts, doctors, and scientist all befuddled. Each person explored ways to help cope or remain sane.

I had a desire to write and put my feeling on paper. Well, it was a blessing in disguise for me. I found I did not have to free up any time. Shut in. cut off from the public, what more could I ask, the opportunity presented itself. I seized the opportunity. I can use much time writing; I am still an amateur. Hopefully, one day I will reach perfection.

It is hard to describe the feelings, mixed emotions. Being afraid, feeling depressed, but hopeful at the same time. I heard a little voice whisper to me, saying "Have a closer walk with a higher power and draw your family in with you. Knowing what was at stake I reached to those close to me. My spouse, my two sons, my sister and brother-in-law, two grandsons, one daughter-in law, one granddaughter-in law, and one first cousin made up our family circle. We did not miss a beat, we gathered for Thanksgiving, Christmas, My 80th Birthday, Mother's Day, and Father's Day. How we did it was very well thought out and executed to a T. All wanted each other to have fun, but also practice safety respecting each other's health and feelings.

We all were:
        Vaccinated, wore masks, sat, ate, and fellowshipped distances apart.
        Washed, sanitized hands and surfaces often. The big question often heard,
        "Did you wash your hands?"

We prayed individually and collectively, meditated daily for the world as well as families. We kept a close tab on each other sharing warnings, suggestions from the experts and using our senses regarding our own health and those around us. We feel blessed that God covered us, and by his grace and mercy we are all alive and hear to share a part of our story.

We never lost sight of the saying, "A Family that Prays Together, Stays Together. We bonded very well and stronger than ever before. LISTEN   PRAY   OBEY

The following poems and articles resulted. I read the BIBLE and used writing to soothe my anxiety. The love and care of my family played a huge part in coping with faith in God.

"Here it is.

Something devastating shocked the world 2021... Can you guess what?

Contagious
Oppressive
Rageful
Omnipresent
Nasal
Airway
Virus
Infectious
Rare
Unbiased
Stressful

Observing citizens in the hospital with the virus, "You don't want this disease." Obey the Doctors, Scientists, and Healthcare Officials. What "YOU" can do is-

Take natural supplements/vitamins to strengthen your immune system; eat plenty of fruits and veggies; wear your mask; wash your hands; distance yourself from a crowd and protect yourself as well as others.

Following these rules, listening to experts may save your life. You have a choice.

'Your life is in your hands." God is in CONTROL.

The Talented Tenacious Ten

The story of ten ladies whose goal was the same
Reaching that goal would bring them fame.
They all buckled down to work extremely hard
Hoping in the end they'd earn more than just a card.
Their sponsors learned more about each of them-
Patricia Baskerville   peaceful, patient, and professional
Joy Carrington   jewel, joyous, and judicious
Jameica Davis   joyful, just jittery and justifiable
Shikee Franklin   smart, slightly shy, but sophisticated
Alethia Gaither   artistic, active but affectionate
Kimberly Jones   kind, knowledgeable, and keen
Hester Mallory   honorable, helpful, hopeful
JoAnne Singleton   just, jubilant, and joyful
Belinda Thompson   bright, bold, and businesslike
Michelle Wright   magnificent, model, and multitalented.
The ladies have all reached their goal
And prepared to take their role
Now they can claim their fame
The word Soror in front of their name.
To this outstanding, great sorority, we're glad they came.

STAY HOME

Home, the place you want to be
Covid 19 changed the meaning of
A place we must be by decree
Or suffer devastating consequences.

Originally, huddling together was desired
Mandated by authority causes hate
Separation at about six feet apart
Now a day doesn't seem smart.

Down the road unknown how far
So many uncertainties a mystery
The waiting, watching will make history
Researchers, inventors sure to be stars.

By the time a vaccine is invented
"Trust God" and ride out this STORM.

Seek More Guidance

For as long as we matriculate on this earth, we will need guidance. In all that we do or say guidance is essential. Who will be the source of the advice is worth much consideration? Should advice come from someone of benefit to you and worthy of listening to? " Caution" is it a wolf in sheep clothing: is it a person of good rapport, respectful and honest? In these perilous times, it be who's you to take no changes. One thing, I know Jesus has worked for me. I encourage you to seek more guidance and from one who has all answers.

Excerpts from the scriptures to think about.

Whether you turn to the right or turn to the left, your ears will hear that small voice behind you saying, This is the way, walk in it. Isaiah 30: 25.

For this God is our God for ever and ever; he will be our guide even to the end.

Psalm 48: 14 or 141

In his heart a man plans his course, but the Lord determines his steps. Proverbs 16: 9.

The Lord delights in the way of a man whose steps he has made firm. Psalm 37:23

His God instructs him and teaches him in the right way.

In all your ways acknowledge him and he will make your paths straight, Proverbs 3: 6

The Lord will instruct us and teach us in the way we should go. He will counsel and watch over us. God promised that he will lead the blind by the way they have not known, along unfamiliar paths, I will guide them; I will turn the darkness into light before them and make the rough places smooth. These are the things I will do, I will not forsake them. Isaiah 42:16

God is always with you, you hold me by my right hand. "Hold to God's unchanging hand and you will not go wrong.

Visionary

Is your vision one of unlimited possibilities?

Jesus was always able to perceive the abundance of God in every place and in every situation.

He had spiritual insight and used it in all situations. (omnipresent)

Jesus taught his disciples about divine abundance as he guided them to feed five thousand people with only five loaves of bread and two fish.

Before breaking the bread so that it could be distributed, Jesus first turned to God in gratitude. He gave thanks to God in prayer. His faith in God gave him a vision beyond the appearance of what seemed too inadequate to feed so many.

Short's Chapel Church and friends, "Let's follow Jesus' example." First, give thanks to God for unlimited possibilities. Ask God in faith and it's yours for the asking. Then move forward with faith. believing with all your heart that all things are possible through Christ Jesus. Love God, he loves you (unconditional). Know with all your heart that God will provide for you. He provides for us whether we deserve it or not. He is a good God, better to us than we are to ourselves. Trust God, and have faith. Be steadfast and immovable---

Taking the five loaves of bread and two fish, he looked up to heaven, and blessed and broke the loaves... And all ate and were filled." Mark 6: 41- 42.

As a Church we can do many things in faith. "Do we all have a vision?

A Roast to Mrs. Helen Green

If you would ask Mrs. Helen Green, "What was your profession?" In an authoritative, firm voice she would say Teacher/ Educator. We are proud of our Profession. This response In itself lets you know the perimeter extends a great distance. This job encompasses a whole arena of other occupations. It paves the way for all other professions. Anyone who has been successful was touched by a teacher in some ways.

Perhaps, Mrs. Green has been a guiding light in someone's life. She may have given a word of encouragement to that quiet. shy child: maybe counseled that child who lacked discipline behaviorally and academically. I know she imparted knowledge and used her wisdom in daily delivery of instructions.

Mrs. Green stepped on a few toes, but stepping on those toes made that boy or girl take a self-inventory and turned out to be a better or more productive citizen.

In order to better herself, she received her masters from Columbia University. She taught for many, many years. Social Studies was the area for which she was the expert. Carrying her students to faraway places without ever leaving the classroom. "Oh the places they visited."

One activity the students would always remember, they had to draw a United States flag that looked exactly like Mrs. Green's flag. She told them "you can draw", "I know you can."

To keep in step with her belief, she joined the first Greek lettered women organization, Alpha Kappa Alpha Sorority. Inc. She was a faithful dedicated member, supported all of its programs providing service to all mankind. She was a cooperative member and served a chairman of various committees. Locally she was affiliated with Gamma Lambda Omega Chapter in Lawrenceville, Virginia.

Mrs. Green is of service and supports Saint Paul's College when she received her Bachelor's Degree. Mrs. Green is an alumni 100% financially and programmatic.

Accolades to Mrs. Green for a job well done. I am proud to be a part of giving your flowers while you live or can smell them.

Faithfulness

Faithfulness is loyalty, trustworthiness, steadfastness. It is characteristic of the person who is reliable. It applies to Christian behavior in respect to people as well as God. God calls women to be faithful to all things.

The marks of faithfulness: A woman walking by the spirit would follow through on whatever she has to do.

Come through   no matter what

She delivers the goods whether - a message or a meal

She shows up   even early so others won't worry

She keeps her word   her yes means yes no means no.

She keeps her commitments and appointments -you won't find her canceling.

She successfully transacts business carrying out any instructions given to her.

She discharges her official duties in the organization and doesn't neglect them.

She is devoted to duty just as Jesus was when he came to do his father's will.

In light of this list, take a quick inventory of your own Christian walk. Let these points stretch your understanding of the fruit of faithfulness, a fruit that is so needed in the world today. I ask God for His strength so we can go to work cultivating His faithfulness in our lives.

By Elizabeth George -Growing in the fruit of the Spirit.

MADELYNE W. RIVERS

Madelyne gone too suddenly
Yesterday slipped by quickly
But her tomorrows will never come again.
We met in the blink of the eye
But loosing her so abruptly certainly made me cry.
We were unable to say goodbye
Friendships should never be taken for granted
For we never know when we'll leave this planet.

I can reflect on those good old memories
A few of them we cherished were..
Dinning out at various eateries, fellowshipping often
We valued and took advantage of these precious moments
Communicating on the phone or dropping a note in mail
No signal nor indication she was going home.
My genuine friend was wonderfully known
Full of laughter, talkative and jovial.

Her last note in a card to me was...
"Thank You"

The goodness and generosity you share
So happily are wonderful reminders of
The true meaning of God's love.
"Thank you for being the blessing you are
To all who know you.

A Tribute to All Mothers

Over and over again we highly favored. So many blessing of which one of them is being a mother. Motherhood brings with it precious gills from God, children. Provisions for Children's needs are a tremendous responsibility. Feeding children when they are hungry, washing and keeping them and their clothes clean, kissing and attending to their hurts and making them fee; better. A mother's touch can do so much. It is a cure all for that ails children. Mothers guided by the holy spirit, having Jesus in their lives, and a strong connection with God makes the job much easier.

A mother reads to her children when she feels like it and even when she does not feel like it. The Bible has instructions for her on what to do and how to do it. It is also a good book to read with children. Many good lessons and parables to learn from.

One such commandment is "' train up a child in the way he/she should go and they will not depart from it. One commandment to the children "respect and obey your elders, parents so that your days many be longer. This adds to the children's lives and also the parents. The Lord commands us to love one another, love our neighbors as ourselves which is the greatest commandment. Mothers have that unconditional love as God does. He loved us so much that he gave his life for us. Mothers will do the same, "die" for her children.

Those of us with mothers living today, "love and respect them." Once they've deceased they will not return physically. Others of us whose mothers have gone to their eternal home, " cherish their memory."

A mother is a virtuous woman, for her price is far above rubies, she is priceless.
Virtuous - upright, good morals, worthy, righteous
Rubies   rare gems, precious stone, expensive
Priceless - beyond price, money can't buy, extremely valuable
God has left the instructions. Will you choose to follow them or not follow?

He Will Counsel And Watch Over Us

As long as we matriculate on this earth, we will need guidance. In all that we do or say, guidance is needed essential. Who can you get guidance from? Consider the source, "is it someone for your good or worthy of listening to?" "Caution" is a wolf in sheep's clothing. Is it a person of good rapport, respectful, and honest? In these perilous times, it's challenging to know. One sure thing "I do know" Jesus has worked for "me". Seek More Guidance. Excerpts for various scriptures.

He promised he will lead the blind in ways they have not known. Along unfamiliar paths, I will guide them: I will turn the darkness into light before them and make the rough places smooth. These are the things I will do: I will not forsake Isaiah 42:16

President Barack Obama

President Barack Obama is truly intellectual

Sent by God every step of the way

Stylish, Mr. personality and skilled rhetorically

Superb communicator with words appropriately to say.

His adversaries couldn't make him mare his character

Accusations hurled his way, no go

Name calling, lying on him and so much more

For whom God touches, no man can hinder.

Their goal was to make him a onetime president

The right side treated him as if he were a germ

The citizens re-elected him to a second term

His Godly ways and action turned out to be evident.

Obama was able to move through Obamacare

The senate blocked practically everything else

Thank God, this "Big" one helped millions fare

An honorable president dedicated to serving.

THE FIRST AFRICAN American President survived despite of all the obstacles.

A tribute to Fathers

Christianbook.com blog says very well a message I voice the sentiment on the message to Christian Fathers.

The message is best said using scriptures from the Holy Bible. The message refers to Godly dads and husbands. The passages selected declares what God intended for men and an honorable way to celebrate our fathers.

My father was firm, stern and seasoned with love unconditionally in his discipline of his children. He worked hard caring for his family. He informed us that as for him and his household WE will serve the Lord. The following scriptures are passages he held fast to raising his children. My father grew up in a Christian home using principles and various teachings in the bible.

Jeremiah 17: 7 – Blessed is the man who trusts in the Lord, and whose hope is the Lord.

Proverbs 17: 6 - Children's children are the crown of old men; and the glory of children are

their fathers.

Proverbs 20: 7 – The righteous who walk in his integrity – blessed are his children after him!

Psalm 103: 13 -- As a father has compassion on his children so the Lord has compassion on

those who fear him.

Proverb 23: 24 – The father of a righteous son will rejoice greatly, and one who fathers a wise

son will delight in him.

Ephesians 6: 4 – Fathers do not provoke our children to anger, but bring them up in the

      discipline and instruction of the Lord.

Joshua 1: 9 – Have I not commanded you? Be strong and of good courage; do not be afraid,

      nor be dismayed, for the Lord your God is with you wherever you go.

Proverb 22: 6 – Start children off on the way they should go, and even when they are old, they

      will not turn from it.

These commandments that I give you today are to be on your hearts. Impressed them on your children, talk about them when you sit at home and when you walk along the road, when you lie down and when you get up. Tie them as symbols on your hands and bind them on your forehead. Write them on the doorframes of your houses and on your gates.

Serving Mankind in a Perilous Time

A Young DJ TRENDING TOPIC KEANE.

This talented young man uses his musical skills

To soothe souls or minds of a hurting society

Bewildered, streaming, and frustrated community.

He turned to what he grossly loves and enjoys

To address those feelings during Covid 19

And to provide others with an outlet and way out.

What a blessing it is that he would serve others,

Sacrificing his own anxiety, time as well as energy.

As prayers go up blessings shower down

As music is played emotions are calmed

But God uses a creative positive young adult

To do a necessary huge task, amid this storm.

With the blink of an eye, maturity evolved.

Is not that God, He works things out for HIS children?

Keane's foundation and teachings were laid early in life

Importantly so, training must line-up with your living'

Devastation, Chaos, catastrophe, and pandemic

Can bring the best or the worst action in such situations.

Keane responded in the best viable way , I am thankful

To God for his marvelous performance in a time like this.

JESUS WORKING FOR HIS GOOD!!

My Grandma (Grace)

By Kyle Thompson

This is how my 9 years old grandson describe me.

He entered a Nestle Very Best reading

Who is your role model?

The lady I would like for you to become acquainted with is five feet and ten inches tall. She is brown skinned and pleasingly plump, 195 pounds. Her hair is not bad but requires a light pressing. It can be easily styled to your satisfaction.

God is my first role model and Grandma is my human role model. God sent her to me and to do a job with children. She has a magical touch with her hands that soothes and make things feel better. She stands tall in any situation and not just in height alone.

If I had to rate grandma on a scale of 1 to 100. I would give her 100. My reason for this high rating is because she is a giant. Saint Paul's College student gave her the name "Amazing Grace," I agree because the things she does and can get done are enormous. She sticks with you through the thick and the thin, the good and the bad.

Grandma Grace is an inspiration to me and many other students. She is not going to tell you anything wrong.

Kyle was I of 32 students in nation that won the contest. Kyle and his family including Grandma Grace enjoyed an all-expense trip to Los Angeles California for 1 week in 1999. Kyle was the youngest student. Nine at that time.

Rita

Proven to be a valued student-friend

Acquainted with since grade six

We endured alarming encounters

Through the highs and the lows

The ups and the downs

The good and the bad

Even deaths and many lives.

Yet thirty years later still connected.

Credit is owed to Rita's parents

Who called it for what it was.

I still applaud them for standing with me

And being the wind that stirred our direction

In the sunshine and in the rain or heart ache and pain

Today, our friendship solidly remains grounded in love.

My 2021 Rita…

Reliable

Intelligent

Thoughtful/ terrific

Ambitious

MATURED INTO A STRONG BLACK CARING WOMAN

I thank God that our paths crossed   and I hold a special place in my heart for Rita.

Kamala Harris

Kamala Harris, my brand of a lady

Matriculated at a top-level University

Charted her course of essential study

A place where her training was authenticated.

Weighs comments often hurled at her

Evaluating who said it or who was the messenger

Criticism screened for its intent or value

Is it worth considering, worthless or beneficial?

Is the source important to the platform or initiative?

Kamala, a woman, sophisticated and very intelligent

Affiliated with positions and organizations, top notched

Guides her in what, when, where and how to respond.

Utilizing integrity, wisdom and discretion.

Listen: the first Black Woman Vice-President of the United States.

Member of the first Greek letter organization of college-educated women

Guided by its ideas and bonded together by love, finances and service.

Kamela Harris is my Greek sister of the AKA Sorority "We have your back"

www.ingramcontent.com/pod-product-compliance
Lightning Source LLC
Chambersburg PA
CBHW060333130626
46553CB00003B/1000